FRIENDS OF JESUS

BY

BETTY SMITH

Illustrated by   CICELY STEED

LUTTERWORTH PRESS · GUILDFORD, SURREY

Fifth impression 1982

STORIES OF JESUS

A beautiful new series of picture books, in which the great story is retold very simply and faithfully. Betty Smith is an Australian who has done much distinguished work for Sunday Schools and Christian education. Cicely Steed is one of the foremost illustrators of children's books, and her pictures with their clear outlines and rich colour are seen at their best in this series.

1 BABY JESUS   3 STORIES JESUS TOLD

2 THE BOY JESUS   4 FRIENDS OF JESUS

5 PEOPLE JESUS LOVED

6 JESUS AND THE CHILDREN

7 JESUS THE HEALER

8 JESUS, KING OF KINGS

BETTY SMITH

ILLUSTRATED BY CICELY STEED

ISBN 0 7188 1670 1

Printed in Hong Kong by Colorcraft Ltd.

CONTENTS

Cicely Steed.

THE MAN WHO CLIMBED A TREE

ZACCHEUS lived in Jericho. When he was young, other boys teased him because he was so small. He was hurt and unhappy. When he grew up, he became a tax-collector (or publican, as they were called). The Romans ruled the land. People had to pay taxes to them. They hated doing this and they hated the men who collected the money.

Zaccheus didn't mind. Now *he* could hurt the people who had made him unhappy. He would tell a man his tax was higher than it really was. Then he would keep the difference. He grew rich and became chief tax-collector, but he was still sad and lonely. He knew that he was doing wrong.

One day, there was great news. Jesus was coming to Jericho. Everyone had heard of Him. Zaccheus thought he would like to see this Prophet (as some people called Jesus). He set out early. To his surprise, crowds already lined the road. Zaccheus was so short that all he could see were people's backs.

"I won't see Jesus at all," he thought. "I must stand in the front."

When the others saw Zaccheus, they said among themselves,

"Here's that tax-collector who cheats everyone. Stand close together so that he can't get through."

They called him horrible names, too, and were so angry that Zaccheus moved. A little further along, he tried again. The same thing happened. No one would let him through.

He was very un-happy. He really *had* wanted to see Jesus. Sadly he leant against a tree.

Then he had an idea. He looked at the tree. It was a sycamore. It would be easy to climb. Tucking his robe around him, Zaccheus jumped. Soon he was hidden among the leaves. He had a grandstand view of a party of men walking towards him.

"This is a good place," he thought. "I'll see Jesus through the leaves and He won't see me at all."

People lining the road were waving and calling as Jesus passed. Now Zaccheus could see His face. Then, just as the men were level with the tree, their Leader halted. He looked up and His eyes met those of the little man in the tree.

Zaccheus felt that those eyes saw all that was in

his mind. They saw his past life and all that he had done. Those eyes seemed to say: "I know all about you — and I'm sorry." He felt so ashamed. Then Jesus spoke,

"Zaccheus! Hurry up and come down. I am staying at your house to-day."

Zaccheus could hardly believe his ears. Jesus knew his name, though they had not met before. The One whom all Jericho had waited to see, was coming to *his* home. Slipping and sliding, Zaccheus climbed down. He didn't wait even to straighten his silken robe. Bowing to Jesus, he said,

C. Steed

"My house is in this street. Please follow me."

Proudly he led the way. He was so happy that at first he didn't hear what people were saying:

"Fancy Jesus going with *that* man!"

"Surely there are plenty of *good* people who would be glad to have Him."

"*He* can't be such a good man if He goes with someone dishonest."

Then Zaccheus heard the remarks. They were talking about Jesus, who had spoken so kindly.

It was all his fault. He stopped and turned around. Then, loudly, so that everyone could hear, he said, "Master, I am going to give half of all I own to the poor."

There was a murmur of surprise, but Zaccheus went on,

"And if I have taken anything from any man wrongly, I'll make it up to him four times over."

Now Jesus was smiling. His eyes said, "Well done! Everything will be right with you now."

Zaccheus felt so happy. He would follow God's way always. Then the crowd heard Jesus say,

"You must remember that God has not sent Me

only to good people. Those who have strayed away from Him must be helped too. Through Me, they can find the way back to God."

"Like me," thought Zaccheus. "Just like me!"

"Jesus passed through Jericho. And there was a man, Zaccheus, chief among the publicans. He sought to see Jesus, but could not, because he was little of stature. He ran before and climbed a sycamore tree. When Jesus came he looked up and said, 'Zaccheus, make haste and come down, for today I must abide at thy house.' And he came down and received him joyfully. And they all murmured, and Zaccheus said, 'Lord, half of my goods I give to the poor' ... Jesus said, 'This day is salvation come to this house. For the Son of man is come to seek and save that which was lost."

Luke 19: 1—10

THE SISTERS AT BETHANY

MARY and Martha were sisters, but they were very, very different.

Martha was the elder. She was really the kindest person and did all she could to help others. When people were in trouble, they always sent for Martha. Everyone knew they could depend on her. But — she was just a *little* too fond of telling others what to do. She was very good at housework, cooking, nursing and sewing. She rather looked down on those who weren't clever at such things. She felt everyone should be just like herself.

"People shouldn't sit around with their hands folded," she used to say.

That was the trouble. For Mary didn't like doing any of the things Martha loved. No, not housework, cooking or even sewing. She was quiet and rather shy. She liked reading. She liked to sit and think. She liked to hear people talking. The person she liked most to listen to was Jesus.

The sisters lived with their brother, Lazarus, in the little town of Bethany. Tucked away in a fold of the hills, it was quiet and peaceful. Jesus and His disciples often paid a visit there to their three friends.

They felt it was almost like a second home to them.

It had been some time since the sisters had seen Jesus. Then He sent word that He was arriving the next day. Martha and Mary were very excited.

From early morning, Martha worked. First, the house must be spotless. Then the evening meal must be prepared. Nothing was too much trouble for Jesus. By the time the guests arrived, she was tired out.

Her brother took Jesus and the others out to the terrace. Here trees made a pleasant shade. The breeze blew softly on their hot faces. Presently, Jesus began to talk to them about their work for God.

Mary listened. Soon she came nearer and nearer. Then she sat down close to Jesus. What He was saying was so wonderful, she quite forgot Martha wanted her help. Time slipped by.

Inside, Martha was getting more and more hot and cross and worried.

"Be careful, you'll burn the meat," she said to one serving girl, then to another,

"What ARE you doing? You know you must use the best bowls on the table tonight. Nothing but the best is good enough for the Master. And where is my sister? Do you know?"

"I think she is out on the terrace, mistress."

Martha felt very ill-used.

"*I'd* like to hear the Master talking too," she thought, "but someone has to do the work. Why doesn't she come and help?"

So she kept fretting and fuming. Every little while she went to the door and looked out. There sat the man and there sat Mary. Martha went back to her kitchen. Her head ached and she felt so hot. Mary was out in the cool breeze. It wasn't fair, Martha told herself. At last, she could stand it no longer. She walked to the terrace,

"Master," she said abruptly. "Don't you care that my sister has left me to do all the work? Tell her to come and help me."

Mary sprang to her feet. She hung her head. Imagine having to be told to help! She felt very guilty.

Jesus looked at Martha. He knew it was because she loved Him so much that she wanted everything just right. He spoke very gently,

"Martha, dear Martha," He said. "You're so busy and worried over all these tasks. But, you know, they don't really matter so much. The things of God are more important. Mary has chosen to put these first."

It was Martha's turn to feel ashamed. Her anger died away. She saw how thoughtless she had been. In future, she would try to fuss less over little things. She would try not to be quite so house-proud.

It was strange, she thought. A moment before she had felt that her work was very important indeed. Now Jesus had helped her to see that God must always come first in the lives of everyone.

"A woman named Martha received him. She had a sister called Mary, which sat at Jesus' feet and heard his word. Martha was cumbered with much serving and said, 'Lord, dost thou not care that my sister hath left me to serve alone? bid her help me.' Jesus said, 'Martha, Martha, thou art careful about many things. But one thing is needful: and Mary hath chosen that good part.'" Luke 10: 38—42

THE MAN WHO LENT HIS ROOM

JOHN MARK lived in the city of Jerusalem. Passover week was here again. John Mark loved this Feast. It helped the people of the land where Jesus lived to remember that God had saved them from slavery long years before.

On the morning of the feast day itself, the household awoke early. Young John Mark wandered from room to room. He felt in everyone's way. Then he heard Father call,

"John Mark! Run and ask Amos to come to me."

Amos had been with the family for years. He was in the central courtyard.

"Amos!" the boy called. "Father wants you."

John went with Amos to the room where Father waited, looking grave. Mother was there, too.

"Amos," Father said, "I'm going to ask you to do something rather strange."

"Yes, Master?"

"I want you to walk through the streets, carrying one of our tall water jars on your shoulder."

Amos stared at Father. "But that's women's work. No man ever does *that.*"

"I know," Father said. "That's *why* I want you to do it. Listen! This is for Jesus."

"Oh, that's different," said Amos.

"You know He's in danger? That men in high positions wish to kill Him? He wants somewhere safe to eat the Passover with His friends. We have arranged for them to come here."

John Mark was thrilled. Jesus in their house!

"Two of His friends — Peter and John — are to help get things ready. They have never been here,

so we made this plan. When they see a *man* carrying a water jar, they will follow him. We have arranged a password. They will say to me, "The Master asks where is the room where I shall eat the Passover with My disciples?"

"Is that because you don't know Peter and John?" asked Mother.

"Yes. After dark, they'll bring the rest of the party to the house."

After Amos left, John Mark asked, "Which room will Jesus use?"

Father said quietly, "We are lending Jesus our upper room. Don't mention this to a single soul."

"I promise," John Mark said.

· The three climbed to the flat roof. The upper room was built in one corner.

"There's not much to do," said Mother. "John Mark, you may fill the water jar."

"I'm just like Amos," John Mark thought.

He climbed back upstairs with the full jar. He was very careful not to spill one drop. Father and Mother had pushed the tables together. Around them were placed the couches on which guests lay. This was the usual custom in those days.

The room was soon ready.

"Peter and John can alter it if they wish,"

Mother said. She walked to the central couch and smoothed the pillow. "I can't believe that in a few hours Jesus will be sitting here."

Father had been standing by the window. Now he turned,

"Mary, I have such a strange feeling. I think that something very wonderful will happen here in our house tonight. Something that the world will remember for ever and ever."

Mother crossed the room and put her arm through Father's.

"I don't understand what it could be," she said, "but if so, what an honour for our home; and all because you lent this room to Jesus."

"He sent Peter and John saying, 'Go and prepare the passover.' And they said 'Where?' And he said, 'There shall a man meet you, bearing a pitcher of water: follow him. And ye shall say to the good man of the house, "The Master saith, where is the guest chamber, where I shall eat the passover with my disciples?" And he shall show you a large upper room, furnished.' " Luke 22: 8—12

THE FRIENDS FROM EMMAUS

THE two walked very slowly. They were tired and full of sadness. Jesus, their friend, had been killed by those who hated Him. It was now the evening of the third day since it had happened. They were going back home to Emmaus.

Over and over, they talked of Jesus' death. They could not believe it was true.

"How could He have been God's Son now He is dead?" one asked.

"I don't know, I just don't know."

"Cleopas, what did you think of the women's story this morning?"

Before Cleopas could answer, they heard footsteps behind them. They looked around and there was another traveller.

"God be with you," He said.

"And with you," they replied, as was the custom.

"What are you talking about?" asked the other man. "You look so unhappy."

Cleopas was surprised at the question,

"Why, sir, you must be a stranger in Jerusalem. Otherwise, you would have heard the things that have happened lately."

"What things?"

"To Jesus of Nazareth. We were His disciples — His friends. He was so good — a real man of God. The priests and rulers hated Him. At last, they told a false story against Him. Three days ago, He was crucified."

The second disciple said gloomily,

"We were so *certain* He was God's Son — the Messiah. Everything pointed to it. But now —"

"There is one strange thing," Cleopas broke in, "Some of the women who loved Him went to His grave this morning. They came running back. They said the body of Jesus had gone."

"Yes, and that they had seen angels," said the second disciple.

"They told the women that Jesus was *alive*."

The traveller had been glancing from one to the other. Now He said,

"Oh, how foolish you are. If Jesus is the Christ,

then all this is exactly what MUST happen. Think of what the prophets have said... that men will turn from the Messiah — that He must die to save the world. Had you forgotten?"

"Please tell us more," begged Cleopas.

So the three walked along in the gathering dusk. The stranger explained everything that had been foretold about God's Son. The two disciples understood as they had never done before.

Soon the lights of Emmaus twinkled nearby. They came to the turn-off. Their fellow-traveller stayed on the main road, as if He were going further. Cleopas spoke quickly,

"Sir, would you care to stay with us? It's late and we would be glad to have you."

The stranger thanked him and they went on together. In the house, they washed the dust from their feet. A meal was prepared. But somehow, Cleopas and his friend began to feel that this was no stranger after all. They sat down and the guest took a piece of bread in His hands. He asked God's blessing. Suddenly, hope flamed in the hearts of the others. Was it possible — could it be — Jesus Himself? Then they saw nail prints in the hands breaking the bread. Falling to their knees, the two bowed their heads.

"Master!"

They looked up, but Jesus had gone.

"How could we have been so stupid as not to have known Him?" Cleopas said. "When He talked with us like that?"

"Perhaps He didn't want us to," said his friend.

"Come, let us go back to Jerusalem and tell the others."

Back to the city the two excited friends hurried with their wonderful news —

"Jesus is *alive*. He walked with us. He talked with us. It's true. He IS the Son of God!"

"Two of them went the same day to Emmaus. While they communed together, Jesus himself drew near and went with them, but they knew him not ... Beginning at Moses and the prophets, he expounded unto them the things concerning himself ... And he took bread and blessed it and gave to them. And their eyes were opened and they knew him." Luke 24: 13—33

32